LOVE IN UPSIDE DOWN WORLD

MANDEEP RANA

Made with ♥ on the Notion Press Platform
www.notionpress.com

Contents

Contents

Contents

Contents

Contents

Foreword

As I sit down to write this foreword, I find myself reflecting on the journey that led to the creation of this poetry collection. Poetry has always been my sanctuary, a place where I can explore the depths of my emotions and give voice to the thoughts and feelings that often remain unspoken.

This collection represents a tapestry of my experiences, observations, and reflections. Each poem is a snapshot of a moment, a feeling, or a thought that has touched me deeply. Through these poems, I have sought to capture the beauty, complexity, and sometimes the pain of life. My hope is that these words resonate with you, the reader, and that you find in them echoes of your own experiences.

The themes in this collection are diverse, yet interconnected. From love and loss to joy and sorrow, each poem is a piece of the larger mosaic of human experience. I have tried to approach each theme with honesty and vulnerability, believing that the most powerful poetry often comes from the heart.

• x •

To you, the reader, thank you for picking up this book and embarking on this journey with me. It is my sincere hope that these poems will touch your heart and mind, and that they will bring you the same solace and understanding that writing them has brought me.

With gratitude,

Mandeep Rana(Author)

Preface

Poetry has long been a valuable tool for delving deeply into the human condition, bringing to life feelings and situations that language is frequently unable to convey. This compilation is a voyage across the mental and emotional landscapes, resulting from a multitude of ideas, experiences, and insights. Every poetry on these pages is a portion of my deepest thoughts, a piece of my soul exposed. They are the outcome of many hours of contemplating the intricacies of joy, grief, love, and loss. I want to provide readers with a mirror to look at their own reflections by expressing the unadulterated, undiluted essence of these universal issues through this anthology.

This collection would not exist without the inspiration and support of many individuals. Writing poetry is an act of vulnerability and courage. It is my hope that these poems resonate with you, the reader, and that you find solace, understanding, or simply a moment of connection within these lines.

Thank you for embarking on this journey with me. May these poems inspire you to look deeper into your own heart and discover the beauty and complexity that lies within.

Acknowledgements

Creating this collection of poetry has been an immensely fulfilling journey, and I am deeply grateful to the many individuals who have supported and inspired me along the way.

First and foremost, I want to express my profound gratitude to my family. To my parents, for instilling in me a love of words and always encouraging my creative endeavors, and to my cousins, siblings, for their constant support and enthusiasm.

To my friends, who have been my first readers and my biggest cheerleaders. Your insightful feedback, unwavering belief in my work, and late-night discussions about life and art have been invaluable.

I also wish to acknowledge my elder brother Mr.Vikash Tomar(Marvelous Poet).You have always been my inspiration and have always shown me the right path and have always stood by me.

Your shared passion and constructive critiques have been a source of inspiration and growth for me.

To my publisher, for believing in my vision and bringing this book to life. Your support has made this dream a reality.

Finally, to my readers. Your willingness to engage with my poetry and find meaning within these pages is the greatest reward. Thank you for allowing my words to become a part of your world.

This book is dedicated to all who find solace and beauty in the power of poetry.

With gratitude,

Mandeep Rana.

Prologue

Published by Notion Press

Description

Many times people say that if you really want to find love, it will come searching for you, if it is in your destiny. But according to me nothing happens like this.

To find the best and true pearl, you have to dive deep into the ocean yourself.

Love is also something like this, like before finding the purest pearl, one or two stones have to be removed and lifted. Similarly, before finding true love, we have to know the people in life. And to find love, you have to do something.

Maybe we know that our life never remains the same forever.But we always try to see everything by standing in one place which limits our scope of vision.

1. Beginning

I Meant....

I Am Alive....

But I Didn't Feel My Heart....

Your memories are the shining lights of literature in the infinite darkness.

@_______________!

"For any question about the book contact me:"
"E-mail: mr.mandeeprana52@gmail.com"
"Instagram:thakurmandeeprajput"
"Twitter: ThakurMandeepR3"
"Facebook: Thakur Mandeep Rajput"

2. Chapter-1 Heart's Content

My heart made my eyes red, I did not even cry.
I got scared looking in the mirror who is sitting so
quite.....

3. Poem 1

Today, my heart is heavy, there is sad peace and silence..

The night is lonely in aspects, but it also has its limits...

I have given him back her life, but there is still a cost...

This is a wound of healed wounds...the pain is still fresh.

4. Notion 1

How much loss do we have to suffer to find love...
We have to live every day and worry about our lives
every day....

5. Poem 2

Tell her not to waste her tears.
Don't tell me the stories of my love.
Now only her memories are in my hand.
Don't tell me who is in her hand.

Now after her even I am not in me.
Now no one should swear on my love.
Now I have no regrets about my condition.
Now no one should take responsibility of me in the
days to pass.

Now empty all the pages of my books.
Now just save my ink for her.
I have waited too long for her.
Tell her not to come even in my dreams now.

Who is responsible for the tears in my eyes now?
No one should take responsibility of the tears in her

eyes.
After that someone tell me now don't waste your life
behind her.

• 6 •

There are so many wounds on my soul.
Now don't apply any balm of love on them.
You never passed through me...
Why should I take the responsibility of passing
through after you.

6. Notion 2

I have stayed awake at night and seen the condition of my eyes.
Still I have never uttered your name in front of anyone.

7. Poem 3

One dark night is left in me.
I am the bright companion of the moon's reflection.
I have a small smile in me.
I live with it.

I am a firefly, witness of a moonlit night.
I am the sleep of the awakened night.
I am the love of an incomplete love.
There is no trace of light in me.

I am the desolate road of the night.
I am the feeling of a sulking love.
I am the moon of the winter night.
My life is as bright as the new moon night.
The full moon has surrounded me in darkness.

My life is like a dewy tree.
Spring is my hope.

My life is like a bird.
Why am I related to a forest?

A light has awakened in me.
Our talk is still left.
The day has passed in memories.
One night is still left.

8. Notion 3

I am a poet; I have to bring light to my life after finding darkness in it.

9. Poem 4

Don't ever apply ointment on my wounds of the heart...

Don't remind me of you when my breaths are slow...

Don't come again to test my pride in the stubbornness of your life...

In this empty life without you... don't light the lamp again...

Tell me my part in the death of the crime of love...

Don't ever grieve for my fading breaths

Grief is life, love is immortal in the silence of death.

The cold winds will turn the sky red as if the path will go incomplete when I leave... come to meet me again...

When the fragrance of your absence will touch my lifeless body...

10. Chapter-2 Existence

I am writing down our story by becoming a stone...
After you, I am taking your oaths to myself...

11. Poem 1

I liked the slight pressure in your eyes...
I liked the way you looked into my eyes...
I liked the way you said sorry from your heart....
I liked the way you smiled calling your love as friendship...

I liked the way you walked away from me while being yours...
I liked the way she hung up his call after seeing me...
I liked the way you stopped while calling me...
I liked the way I stopped before making promises of love to someone...

I liked the way my fight with myself broke down one day...
I liked the way I went away from you being upset...
I liked the way you met me being upset... and the way you left without saying anything...

12. Notion 1

Is there any spell that will make everyone forget about our existence?

13. Poem 2

I think something might happen across my chest.
I think something will happen to me my friend..
After that, what should I do with my condition?
Let me see her once to my heart's content...
And after that, friend, something will happen to me...

Now it is difficult to dwell on her memories...
Man, may something happen to her memories after me...
The loneliness of being in a closed room is beginning to overwhelm me.
After me, something should happen to the loneliness of my work.

Just like waking up at night with black eyes....
Friend, may something happen to my eyes after me..
Whatever words are left between us...
Friend, after we part, something might happen to

my words...

I have changed the path of my destination...
After me, there should be someone on my destination.
What will happen to the vows I took after you?
After me, friend, may something happen to the vows I have taken.

I will go again one day at a time..
After me, may something happen to my loved ones...
May everyone get the reason for everyone's love...
Friend, no one should be left alone after me..

14. Notion 2

My breathe had a better understanding of your soul...

My heart had created a spectacle for no reason...

15. Poem 3

Sweet love, sweet dreams, you are more mine than the beloved
There will be sweet talks...
There will be some days, some nights
Then the time to meet may come...
Some may come slowly, some may come quickly.

There will be the beginning of a new love...
There will be some talks, some memories...
In the sun-scented stretch...
There will be some talks of me, some of you, some of being one

*We will keep growing day by day.. We will make a
new relationship...
We will keep some friendship, some love, some new
rituals. Slowly, love will also happen...
In some days, some nights,
we will confess our love...*

*Slowly we will be together...
Some of it will be soul and some of it will be
physical...
You will be in the fragrant lanes of my heart...
You will get lost some moments with me...*

*The night is about to get intoxicated...
You will fall asleep in my arms...
Narrow streets and small dreams...
Then we will be confined to them...*

*Gradually the distance will increase...
You will not be able to fulfill your vows of not going
away.
Will you be able to cry in front of me...
Will you be able to cherish the relationship again?*

Will you go away from me.. .
Then my love will be incomplete...
Then it will be complete here only with the rituals of
some poetries, my friend.
I will be left alone even in this endless universe...
My friend, I will not be able to live without you.

Well you will feel that all this is old news..
Now who can die for anyone?
Will anyone be able to maintain such kind of
relationships..

My love rituals are different...
But how will you understand them...
know my condition... who will tell you all this.

You come to see me again...
I swear to you...
Don't let your eyes get wet...
I will come to you in your dreams one day.

You will also yearn for my memories...
Some will be incomplete and some will be complete...
But I will not be able to meet you again...
I will be very far away...

You come to meet me at the grave...
Bring some red roses too...
I will calm down again...
I will sleep peacefully again...

Come back from my grave...
You will make the world a new place...
Don't let your love go...
Support someone from your heart...

Whatever happened to me, you know...
Be respectful to yourself...
You have left some fireflies of your memories with me...
You can create a new world again...

16. Notion 3

The darkness of the dark nights consumed me too. Every day I saw myself as something else in the awakening enthusiasm.

17. Poem 4

The day seems heavy
If I sleep, the night goes out of control..
I don't know when I will remember my beloved...
If I don't wake up, the conversation remains
incomplete...

You are the song of my music...
If I see you in my dreams...
Then the memory goes out of control...
Whenever I am in her memories.
My conversation with her remains incomplete...

You are the song of my heart, my love
If I don't reach you...
The rhythm remains incomplete...
Leaving all the ties of home, my love

You come to meet me
You take all my resentment and go back home in the
evening.

18. Chapter-3 Autumn

What should I say about the rooms of my house after you...
My heart and walls scream and tell me that I am alone...

19. Poem 1

Then I remembered the stories of my first love.
Then I remembered the broken pieces of my heart.
The pain of my heart's sight was reflected in my eyes.
Then I remembered some of my things left behind.

The time of my romance with you was strange.
Then I remembered some responsibilities and some dreams.
The years spent with you came to my mind in a moment.
Then some moments remained incomplete and some promises came to my mind.

20. Notion 1

As the night approaches, I drive myself crazy. With each passing day you are becoming less and less.

21. Poem 2

I wrote for someone and kept telling someone throughout my life.
The rest was your name which kept humming in my heart in silence.
It was the night of union in which I accepted separation.
But a drop of my eye kept calling me unfaithful.

I kept taking the blame for the destruction of our love, but
It was a drop of your eye which kept calling you unfaithful.
I am not the only one responsible for the nights of separation that I spent.
I kept maintaining relationships by swearing not to hurt anyone's heart all my life

22. Notion 2

I lost myself in her separation. You did not love me truly even when we met...

23. Poem 3

You left me alone on the burning roads with the support of loneliness,
The smile on my sad face is still there, it is still stubborn to keep me alive even after you.
I have set out to bet with the sea with my army.

24. Notion 3

Who knows how long the love vows will last..

I want to see how much my love will bear.

25. Poem 4

We will be separated from you without talking.
Without you, my paths remained incomplete.
Without you, we will not be able to walk on them.

There was a time when these paths met every moment.
In my hopes, some path will collide.

These memories of mine will torment me.
When your memories will rain on me in the form of drops.

This wind, this rain, this autumn season.
Becoming your memories, they will dissolve in me.

I have spent this time without you.
In a few years, I will also pass away.

Those seasons of friendship according to you.
Those seasons will also leave us.

In a few years, we, this city of yours.
Will be separated from each other.

These heavy sleeps in the little eyelids.
You will be visible in my sleep.
You will collide with me on the path of my dreams.

26. Chapter-4 Illusion

When someone falls in love then a love story is created, when someone fulfils their love then a fairy tale is created...

27. Poem 1

How can I promise to be with you
An incomplete yet complete conversation is yet to be
told...

How can I promise to love you
An incomplete love story is yet to be heard...

How can I promise to migrate...
If she is not there, then nothing is left in me...

How can I confess to you.
There is only one night left in me...

How can I promise the mornings...
A love story is yet to be told...

How can I promise words...
I am a nomad like a firefly of the night...

How can I promise my nights...
How can I complete your conversation...
How can I promise to spend time with you...

I have passed through her...why do you have to come
passed through me...

One thing is left between us, I love her...

This whirlpool is not with us...I want to keep
fighting with this...
How can I promise to be with you...
How can I promise to love...
I have spent every day with her...
How can I walk with you...

We have not been together...
That is why I walk with you...

I have not done business in love...
I will do business with you in love...
How can I promise to be with you...

28. Notion 1

Now I have started remembering you at night again....
My day passes by in a rush again...

29. Poem 2

I came back after turning the road of destruction...
A smoldering fire. Breaking the heart of a poet, I came back...

Now only my room, the narration of my past life comes to mind...
Leaving your name written incomplete in the books of that room, I came back...

The clock knocks on the wall, of every moment of mine,
Writing on the pages of my diary, I came back that hand of time...

Now I think of my busy nights of the past...
Leaving the support of your memories, I came back...

30. Notion 2

Now I don't mind my condition...
Now I've made myself a spectacle...

31. Poem 3

I am thinking of returning to the path of destruction
I should return to mend the smoldering heart of a poet

Now even my lost parts have started searching for me again...I should return to search for those parts myself...

Those stories of ours which were lost in the past have started calling me again...even after you, I should return to search for our memories in those stories...

After you left, seeing your shadow on every knock, I think of returning to call your name on every knock.

This moisture that remains in my eyes every moment...I should return to find the answer to this moisture...

• 44 •

Now even the walls of my room tell me that I am alone...I should return to search for the promises of our friendship in those rooms...

32. Notion 3

Now I am looking for new sorrows
I am starting to feel less troubled again.

33. Poem 4

This illusion should break soon.
This restless mind of mine.

It will get lost in the dark night.
I have tormented myself every night.

Shadows with you.
This illusion will break soon.

Too much light has started piercing my eyes.
Since when have I started liking darkness.

You knew me, right?
Come back to explain something to my eyes.

These four walls. The roof and me.
This dark room. This bright firefly.

This closed cupboard.
And your memories, what should I say.

If you come to meet me, I will tell you about the pain in my eyes.

Without you, it is all sad. Like a fish splashing in the lake, my heart is stuck in the hook of a fisherman's rod, waiting for you.

Just like this river has come out of its banks in search of a confluence with the sea, I also set out like this every day. To leave my footprints in your remaining life.

34. Chapter-5 Desires

My heart which doesn't work as per my wish.
So let it hurt.
Because it loves.

35. Poem 1

Why should I stay in the city of your desires?
Why should I love anyone else other than you?
I haven't even got your memories back yet.
Why should I end this sequence inside me?

My dream, why should we stop you from coming and going?
You said it was our foolishness, now why should I isolate myself from the world ?
Why should we dwell on your memories, why should we cry looking at your pictures.
Why should we read poetries of your name in my college now?

For your sake I did not even keep friendship with you.
Why should I keep flirting with you even in my dreams.
Why should I keep my busy nights dark with the

shadow of your eyelashes.
Why should I share myself with the different parts
of nights.
Why should I wait for you and love you only.

If yes, then I will build your house as the first house
in my heart.
Why should I call that house a home?
Why should I moisten my ghazals with tears of your
name?
When will I keep my sad face away from my face?
When will I fulfill my vows of not making you look
sad?

36. Notion 1

Now even the memories of her are not there in me...

Why am I sad now..

37. Poem 2

I have kept something of mine in the closed room of your memories. Yesterday I opened that room in your memories.

Some of your memories are connected with the winds of unseasonal rain. Yesterday I broke off the ties with these winds without any reason.

The blossom that came in the garden, those paths passed in memories, those benches lying empty without you, that
your city, those days drenched in rain,

your light smile, that shade of the tree, that time of waiting, I remember all your memories.

39. Poem 3

I will always be like you, you always stay like yourself

I will always be with love, you always stay in love

I will always live in your words, you always stay in my words

I will always be lost in your thoughts, you always stay in my thoughts.

I will always be with you like a book, you always stay in me like the pages

I will always be with you like the mountains, you always stay in me like the valleys

I will always be in you from the mountains, you always stay with me like the valleys.

40. Notion 3

Have started calling myself unfaithful...

Ever since she stopped looking at me

41. Poem 4

I think I'll tell you the truth...
Love with me won't be easy
I think I'll make you cry by saying...
That I'm not worthy of you...

I think I'll remind you...
How much I've disgraced you...
I think I'll hug you.
And make myself cry...

I think I'll tell you the truth...
I don't want to be away from you...
I think I'll punish myself...
But I don't want to lose you...

I think I'll show you the truth of love...
I'll kill myself to show you
I think I'll save you from the darkness...
Of course I'll burn myself to show you...

I think I'll tell you the truth...
I've woven some dreams with you.
I wish that my dreams come true...
You are with me...

I wish that I should erase myself...
I wish that I should tell you...
Love with me will not be easy.

42. Chapter-6 Fragrance of Failure

Some of my old loves have surfaced again…
Seeing someone my eyes became moist again..

43. Poem 1

I will not be able to erase your name after writing it.
I will hold your name to my lips.
The pages on which you wrote your name and left.
I will die looking at those pages without taking my breath.

44. Notion 1

*Now the season of her memories is a little upset with
me.*
Now I don't write anything in her memory.

45. Poem 2

Losing the darkness in the nights.
Sleeping alone like this, controlling my breath.
Your innocent face.
Brings back the memories.

Writing so many letters of mine which were not sent
to you.
Removing the darkness from your memories.
Bringing the memories written by you forever.

Writing about you in all the poems.
Becoming the patience of the breaths of the breaths.
Understanding the tears from the hiccups of
memories.
Yes, she remembered me.

Then these November days are numbered.
Changing days into weeks.
Walking together on those old paths.
Will you be able to lose yourself somewhere with me.

46. Notion 2

I thought you understood me. I thought I understood myself with you.

47. Poem 3

I remember her.
It brings the fragrance of roses scattered in water.
What she desires.
The mirror shows my reflection to her.
I remember her.

The edge of her eyelashes brings water.
Which rains drop by drop.

Who decorates the monsoon even in the month of
autumn..
I remember her.

This dark night should awaken her memories in me.
Which should bring the glow of her memories in my
moist eyes.
Just like blue shows its color in water.

Like that her words get absorbed in me
I remember her.

48. Notion 3

Mine for me, from me for me, you are a precious part of me in me.

49. Poem 4

I smile slowly.
I tease the breaths.
The lips are left alone.
I play with the moon and the stars.

When the moonlight dims.
I deny my own happiness.
So that the night does not become lonely.
I absorb her love before the dawn.

Before the sun rises, I empty the mirror.
Knowingly or unknowingly I do not want the
reflection of the face in the mirror to be visible.
I keep the window closed till then.
I deny the light.

50. Chapter-7 Accusation

And I still owe you your memories.
If I meet you again in my next life, I will repay them.

51. Poem 1

I have come walking barefoot in the dew falling in the rainy season

By sharing the fireflies on the path, I have brought darkness inside me...

Like layers are coming off the rusted iron... I have come wounding my own soul like this...

After those dark nights, I am in a bad state..even in that, I have shared the happiness of my deeds with people by clearing their misunderstandings.

The scenes never stung my fearless eyes... Today, I have not been able to store the sorrow of their departure in those eyes...

I had shared love with the hypocrites walking on the roads... Now every hypocrite has come to ask for an account of my love...

52. Notion 1

Nothing else happened.
I did not even get what I wanted

53. Poem 2

After the story ended, regret remained in my eyes
My mind took a boat to some sad seas...

*This story of love has been going on for the past
many centuries*
*Someone's love remained lonely, someone remained
in the desire to live...*

In your promises, my promises did not come true...
*Like every story, in my promises, in this story too, a
person remained alone. In new meetings, there were
no new accusations...*

*In the search of new wounds, some old wound
affected again...*

54. Notion 2

I want to meet you there.
Where I lost myself...

55. Poem 3

You blinked your eyes...

The silence of the closed room has suddenly broken...

The dark night has disappeared somewhere in your deep eyes....

I don't know since when...I am wandering in search of the shade of your eyelids.

56. Notion 3

I want to meet you one last time.
I want you to have some moments with me.

57. Poem 4

Because you did not come....
All the seasons became empty...
The fragrance of your memories could not reach me.
So every season became questionable

The thought of myself did not reach me...
That I got lost in your memories in every season...
If only this throbbing pain of mine would stop....
How would I pass these long nights of separation.

This season, this rain, these cold winds.
Awaken your memories in my moist eyes.
This   mirror,   these   reflections,   these   false

appearances.
The false smile of sad faces.

There are neither nights in the eyes nor mornings in
the days.
Like drops in the rain.
My heart drowns in you.
Such are the beauty in my life.
The stories of your memories

58. Chapter-8 Journey

After you, there will be no one like you.
This form of mine will never be like itself.

59. Poem 1

Again a new morning has begun...
Again a new day is ruined without you...
This is a story from some years ago...
This journey has just begun...

Nights are spent in memories...
You stay without talking..
Hopes are ruined again..
This journey has just begun..

Now I have hope from the darkness...
These moments are with me...
The light is ruined again....
This journey has just begun...

Now I am not feeling well...
It seems I have fever...
This season of rain is ruined...

This journey has just begun...

Now I have an account of my breaths...
This heart is sad without you.
The beating of my heart is ruined...
The journey has just begun...

I have to walk on some path today...
It is the beginning of a turn in my life...
Without you, these paths are ruined
The journey has just begun...

I am waiting for another bus...
Today, your memories are with me in this journey...
Again, your journey is ruined...
The journey has just begun...

Then these moving roads...
This rising sun, these moving winds...
The empty space near me is ruined without you...
The journey has just begun...

I have to meet your city again...
You are not with me again, every moment is sad...
One destination is ruined again...
The journey has just begun...

This heavy sadness in my heart today...
*It is the beginning of separation from my loved
ones...*
Some hearts have fallen out today...
The journey has just begun...

60. Notion 1

Gradually the darkness gave me space.
Then for some days I started stealing light.

61. Poem 2

Having ended one love of mine. .
I keep moving forward.

Having lost one dream of mine.
I keep fighting with myself.

Having lost one sleep of mine.
I want to wake up in the morning.

I have lost one love.
The one which is dearer than you.

Having closed my eyes.
I want to cover the sun.

I am in search of coolness.
I want to climb the moon.

62. Notion 2

You have made a lot of progress now, you have no regrets about the memories now...

63. Poem 3

One Lonely evening is left again.

Your name is left again in me .

Then the series of memories continues .

One unfinished work is left again .

64. Notion 3

I have chosen the night again, someone has come to my mind again.

I am entangled in myself again, someone has hurt my heart again.

65. Poem 4

One victory is equal to you for me
One defeat is equal to my life...

One ritual is equal to you for me...
One tradition is equal to my life.

One love is equal to you for me...
One separation is equal to my life...

66. Chapter-9 Regret

I am remembering you on every infidelity. I am loving you every moment as the days pass by.

67. Poem 1

This second quarter of the night, these slow cool winds blowing... in which the scattered showers of the arrival of the monsoons fell on me, I remembered you....

In these scattered showers, your memory has come to me, I want to touch you with my heart by flowing with these winds...

This cool flow of these winds mixing with the rain awakens your memories... this is how I find moments of your other memories in me...

Why do these memories of yours make me cry... they teach me to live... why do they wake me up in this second quarter of the night... they call me to you... they remind me of you... then they wake me up... they tell me that you are mine...

This rain tells your tone... this wind awakens your memory...

And this not getting mixed in the soil of the rain... tells me that you are not mine... cutting through the soil of the rain and flowing away... you seem to be far away from me...

68. Notion 1

I am like the rain of Monsoon..
Oops...your cold tone is like December.

69. Poem 2

Some love vows were promises...I broke them and fulfilled them..

I said I love her a lot...if you don't want me...then I miss you a lot...

Some promises were broken to myself...some confusion is still there...

I am a bit confused in myself...some memories of you are still there...

Now I have started remembering you again...which is defeating me again...

Whatever oaths I had taken...whatever promises I had made...

Now the blame for them is on me...my not talking to you is one thing...fighting for you is another.

70. Notion 2

After you, I spent many nights waiting for you, my friend.

I don't know how that one night passed in my control, my friend.

71. Poem 3

*I will not be able to erase your name after writing
it....*
I will stick your name on my lips....
*The pages on which you had written your name and
left...*
*I will die looking at those pages without taking my
breath...*

72. Notion 3

Even after you were gone, you were not left alone.

Even after you were gone, there was a fight with you..

73. Poem 4

Some regret for your departure... some regret for my loss

Some memories of yours remained with me... some words of yours remained in my memory...

Some I separated myself from you... some of yours are still left

Some I remembered your words... some of yours I forgot

Some I stayed with you... some you distanced yourself from....

Some time was left with me... some you snatched away...

Some I meant I loved you... some you increased them...

Some I cried being away from you... some you made me cry...

Some of our words are still left... some words you have ended...

Some time I spent with you... some time I was away from you...

Some I grew up with you... some you reminded me of my childhood...

Some I meant I loved you... some you got love from someone...

Some of my hearts were given to you by lovers... one heart you got from a rival...

Some I meant I worked for myself... some you erased me...

Some regret for your departure... some of my words being lost...

74. Chapter-10 Sorrows

I too found happiness in it.
I too had a glimpse of the moon.

75. Poem 1

This time I will go beyond limits....
Will I really love again..

I don't know this...
Will I really have a friend like you....

And after you I am looking for someone like you...
Who will really love me...

This time I will go beyond limits, will I really love again
Now I don't remember you everyday....

Will I really trust anyone..
Will I really fall in love again....

76. Notion 1

The layers of my eyes are getting filled up...
This night is becoming questionable...
Why am I still not able to sleep...
Oh, I remembered...
The date of the days of separation is about to come again...

77. Poem 2

I am lost in your memories while searching for ways to escape the prison of your memories..

Some of your memories are like the personality of the nights... just like the darkness is endless, your memories are like the loan of a shining lamp...

78. Notion 2

You should take a promise from me too.
I will also come in your dreams.

79. Poem 3

How many faces am I making...I am hiding my sorrows...

I am talking to everyone on the oath of being playful with you...

I am composing poetries on meeting you every day...

My love was like Krishna, I am telling you that you are Radha....

I remember even my last meeting with you...I am making pictures with you...

I am spreading myself on your soft breaths...

Seeing you from far, I am talking to you.

Every day I am going to those places where I used to sit with you

Every day I am forgetting you from the memories..

80. Notion 3

Rituals of my love were different.

The story was created after separation.

81. Poem 4

You blinked your eyes...

The silence of the closed room has suddenly broken...

The dark night has disappeared somewhere in your deep eyes...

I don't know since when...I have been wandering in search of the shade of your eyelids..

82. Chapter-11 Memories Poem 1

You like a mild cough.

I want your light eyes closed.

You like light silliness.

I love your little actions.

83. Poem 2

Whenever I start laying the bed,

I start going to the edge of your memories.

Whenever I start going to the edge without you,

I start getting lost at the edge.

I still remember the stories of old memories,

I start forgetting you in the old memories.

84. Poem 3

Something must have happened... you must not have turned into ashes without reason... someone's memories must have been burnt... you must have kept someone's heart...

You must not have listened to yourself... you must have turned your face away from your own desires...

You must have killed some of your own wishes one day.... you must have kept someone's desires...

You must have read your own face by looking at someone's face...

You must have loved someone after killing your own principles...

You must have fought with yourself for me... then you must have cried for someone else...

Then you must have trusted me... whom you must have loved...

Then for a victory... you must have lost me... you must have played a game again...

85. Poem 4

Someone stole my soul or it is lost somewhere. Now its not inside me not there since I am alive and still not living.
Recite such a spell that my soul can reach me.

86. Chapter-12 Soul

My death is my gift, there is nothing in me.

Now no one is looking for you, my dear, my profession.

My lonely showdown in the world. I am a lone traveller.

My destination is no longer on the path of my steps.

The divided parts of my soul got broken and went to someone somewhere.

There is no account of the memories kept within me.

87. Poem 1

I have chosen the night again,

it means someone has come to my dreams again...

I am entangled in myself again,

someone has hurt my heart again.

88. Notion 1

It is not necessary to know someone to love them.

But to leave someone you need to know them very well.

89. Poem 2

Leaving a deep impression on the seasons..

By becoming a cloud and changing the path of the winds

I was learning the art of scattering

I was scattered all my life

By becoming ashes, leaving behind the words of deceit in my heart, I flew into the sky

What will happen to me now with your wandering pictures, you could not even gather the moisture of my heart

I got shattered after clashing with all the loves..

I distanced myself from all the seasons, rivers, deserts and pleasures.

Before you left me, I mourned the death of every hope.

90. Notion 2

I don't even live alone still it is visible through the heavy eyelids of the eyes.

91. Poem 3

All memories fade away, poems become true one day. For fearless eyes, I set out on unknown paths with trembling steps.

The soft breeze comes and goes with the leaves, the song is the same speed, it awakens love in me, it torments my breath, it brings your memories, it wakes me up, it puts me to sleep, it wakes me up.

I have come far away from myself, now even my home is not visible, I don't know where I go, I get scared every evening.

Now all faces seem black, the night's restrictions, the day's guards. My memories, my words, I am lost now, the world knows, now I have turned into stone.

You don't know the truth of words, you don't know the depth of words. How will you find it in me, you don't even recognize your own desires.

I have blossomed into sand particles, many loves have been reduced to stone heart.

92. Notion 3

I don't even live alone still it is visible through the heavy eyelids of the eyes.

93. Poem 4

I am counting the hours in the room for some time. The layers of my eyes are getting filled, still I am writing the red tears of your memories with black ink..

Till the time I heard the final news of your separation from you, my heart did not accept that you had left me somewhere long ago..

Now even the corners of my bed understand my turn, is it sleep or a series of questions of memories...

It is getting long since I met you. Even today the shadows of the photographs are still visible in those places...

There is no coincidence even though we are in the same city, on any road also no face of the old story is ever seen...

94. Notion 4

I have gone through many things in search of love...
Your departure has overshadowed all the search...

95. Resentments

Leave me in the hands of desires. Don't think of me as lost, my loved ones.

I have left myself in the hands of my heart and destiny. You too should leave me in the hands of my resentments.

Whether I feel the pain of my heart or not in my broken dreams, my eyes are still holding on to moisture.

I am awake at night with the help of my sleeping dreams. Still I have run away from the lights and resentments.

Whether it is a dark night or a dark night, I hear the screams from the heart and the walls. How many cities of dreams have burned. What will anyone say when there are lanes of helplessness in the solitudes.

Did I fall asleep or were my eyes filled with tears? The soul trembles thinking about the scenes of dreams. There are some lights that reach the cupboard. There are some windows which are humming the sound of wind in the silence of the room. There are some words which are becoming useless. There are some poems which are making me forget.

Thank you.

Lots of love to all my readers .

Finally I am Alive

@__________________!

96. Suggestion:

Sometimes we match with wrong people that's was we think but you have to gave sometime to your match it should we best match for you than your perfect match

Not everyone has love and those who don't are actually left separated from such a form of life or in other words, they are unable to know the larger form of themselves and the world.

I do not talk about getting love, that is a different thing. If love happens then it is never incomplete, it is a complete thing in itself.

97. View:

I like love stories sometimes i felt that I love those people whose love stories are on the track of success.

At every day night i have to wish a wonderful love story should i create with my loving fellow.

www.ingramcontent.com/pod-product-compliance
Lightning Source LLC
Chambersburg PA
CBHW020544160726
47991CB00002B/577